Cook Memorial Public Library
3 1122 01331 6711

W9-BDV-095

All About Plants

All About
Stems

Claire Throp

Chicago, Illinois

Edited by Claire Throp and Brynn Baker
Designed by Peggie Carley
Picture research by Ruth Blair
Production by Victoria Fitzgerald
Originated by Capstone Global Library Ltd

Printed and bound in China by RR Donnelley Asia

18 17 16 15 14
10 9 8 7 6 5 4 3 2 1

Library of Congress Cataloging-in-Publication Data
Cataloging-in-publication information is on file with the Library of Congress.

ISBN 978-1-4846-0510-3 (hardcover)
ISBN 978-1-4846-0516-5 (eBook PDF)

Acknowledgments
We would like to thank the following for permission to reproduce photographs: Dreamstime: Erikamariag2, 7; Getty Images: WIN-Initiative, 21; iStockphoto: Kurt Drubbel, 11; Shutterstock: Arevik, 14, Filipe B. Varela, 5, gemphoto, 17, gillmar, 8, Igor Borodin, 18, Jane McLoughlin, 19, Krzysztof Wiktor, 20, Maria Skaldina, 6, 23 (top), Max Topchii, cover, Mikhail Dudarev, 4, mythja, 16, 23 (bottom), Rafal Olechowski, 9, Scott Sanders, back cover, 15, 23 (middle), Serg64, 13, smuay, 10, Steve Slocomb, 12, StudioNewmarket, 22

We would like to thank Michael Bright for his invaluable help in the preparation of this book.

Every effort has been made to contact copyright holders of material reproduced in this book. Any omissions will be rectified in subsequent printings if notice is given to the publisher.

006995RRDF14

Contents

What Are Plants?

Plants are living things.

Plants have many parts.

What Do Plants Need to Grow?

Plants need sunlight and **air** to grow.

Plants need water to grow.

What Are Stems?

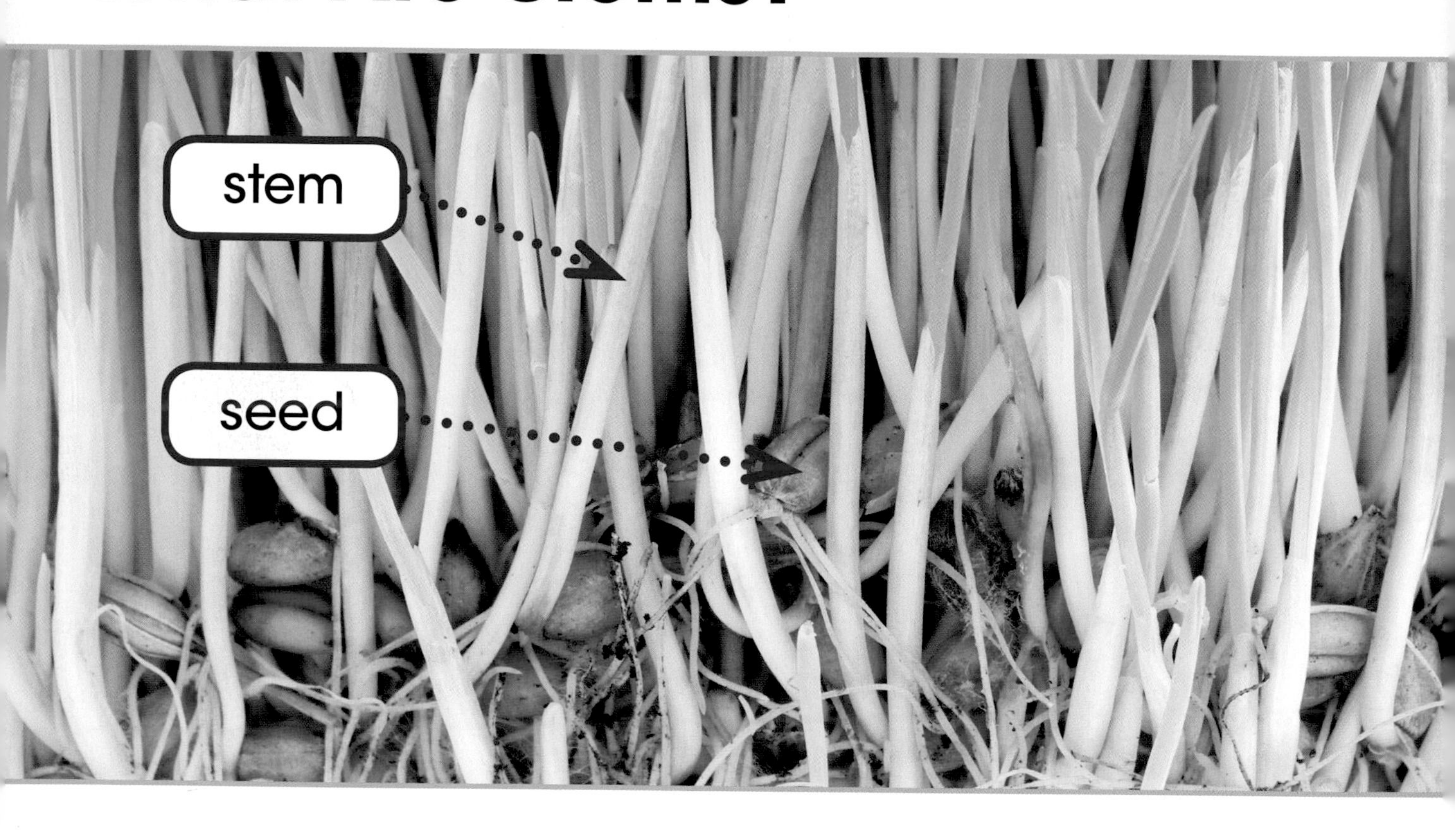

Stems grow from the seeds of plants.

Most stems grow above the ground.
Stems help to hold up a plant.

Stems move water and food around a plant.

Flowers and leaves grow from stems.

Types of Stems

Some plants have thick stems.

Some plants have thin stems.

Some plants have flat stems.

Some plants have **thorny** stems.

Some plants have **woody** stems. A tree trunk is a stem.

Some plants have smooth stems.

Some stems grow along the ground. Strawberry stems grow this way.

Many stems grow straight up.
Rhubarb stems grow this way.

Stems as Food

Some animals like to eat stems.

Some people like to eat stems too. Asparagus is a stem.

Plants Need Stems

Stems hold up plants.
Stems move food around plants.

Picture Glossary

air oxygen people, plants, and animals breathe to live

thorny many sharp, prickly points on a plant

woody made of wood

Index

Notes for Parents and Teachers

Before Reading

Ask children if they know what stems are for. Explain that plant stems can look very different from one another. For example, strawberry runners and tree trunks are very different.

After Reading

- Ask children to say what grows from a stem.
- See if children can remember what three things plants need most to survive. (pages 6 and 7)
- Demonstrate how water moves through stems. Use a white carnation with a freshly-cut stem. Put the flower in a vase with water and food coloring. Ask children to predict what will happen. The colored water will be absorbed by the stem and travel up to the petals. The flower will change color.